# Messages

## from

# Heaven

Anita R. Sneed-Carter

Published in Cedar Hill, Texas by The Sneed-Carter Christian Publication, the Walking By Faith Ministry, and the Walking By Faith Online World Ministry.Org.

Distributed by TSCCP
P. O. Box 701
Cedar Hill, Texas 75106-0701

ISBN LCCN/PCN 978-0-615-70384-8

Cover Design by: The Sneed-Carter Christian Publication

All Scripture was taken from the Holy Bible.

Printed in the United States of America.

*"I can do all things through Christ, who strengtheneth me." ~*

*Philippians 4:13*

*To My Lord and Savior Jesus Christ,*

*This book would not be possible if it were not for the daily indwelling, and powerful filling of your wisdom. You are "**The Author**". It is all about you!*

*This writing experience has been very humbling, encouraging and uplifting. Thank you for the opportunity to serve you Lord, and to be a blessing to many by sharing your written Holy Word.*

*All glory, honor, and praise belong to you!*

~

## ~Dedication~

This book is dedicated in loving memory of my parents, the late Reverend George and Lillie Sneed. I thank and love them for instilling, *"God's Word"*, in me as a child, which led to my receiving Christ as my Savior and Lord at an early age.

Although they are no longer with us on this side, they are resting in the arms of Jesus!

*We are confident, I say, and willing rather to be absent from the body, and to be present with the Lord."* ~

*II Corinthians 5:8*

Love,

*Your Loving Daughter*

## ~Acknowledgements~

Thank you to all of my wonderful Brothers and Sisters in Christ Jesus in the United States, Internationally, Globally, and to all of the readers who support our work and ministry: Adra, Teresa, Bobby, Kim S., Joshua, Arnita, Priscilla, Janine, Kimani, Ethel, Bessie, Mary, Manervia, Sharon, Carrie, Lynn, Maria, Valerie, Steve, Milbourne, Donna, Sonja, Stephanie, Dannielle, Jessica, Meg, Tony.

Also, thanks to: Pastor Tony, Deacon Phil, Pastor Craig, Kimberly B., Shamoon, Roselle, Matheo, and many other beautiful people we have met through the ministry. God bless each and every one of you. ~

Much Love,

*Anita R. Sneed-Carter*

# ~Endorsements for Anita R. Sneed-Carter~

*"Messages from Heaven by, Anita R. Sneed-Carter, is an awesome read. It is a book filled with the love, wisdom and revelation of God. Lives will be touched in every area as readers have an opportunity to experience these messages from Heaven." ~ Review by, Pastor Arnita L. Fields, Author of, "Drop That Bottle, and Pick up a Fork!"*

*"I love this book, (The Man in My Heart), because it is so true to life. As a single woman, I could truly relate. This book would not only be a great book for individuals desiring to gain spiritual, but it could greatly serve as an excellent support guide for single weary women everywhere who truly need to know, and understand that the true man of their heart will come from the Creator. A job well done Minister Anita R. Sneed-Carter." ~ Review by: Adra Young, Author of, "The Everyday Living of Children & Teens Monologues Series"*

*"I was deeply moved by, "The Man in My Heart." Not only touching the heart and soul, but revealing how God brings us through trials and tribulations standing in faith. Her reflections, (Anita), on love and relationships, stimulate awareness and compassion. A true revelation! A must read! I recommend to everyone. Great job Mrs. Anita and I'm looking forward to reading Messages from Heaven." ~ Reviewed by: Cheryl Brandon, Author of, "Inside the Mind of a Poet"*

## ~Other Books by Anita R. Sneed-Carter~
*( Plays Available Summer 2013!)*

## Plays

### Children Christmas Plays
The Sneed-Carter Christian Publication © 1999
Second Edition Revised - © 2012

### The Risen Lord
The Sneed-Carter Christian Publication © 1999
Second Edition Revised - © 2012

### Jesus Christ, He Loves Me?
The Sneed-Carter Christian Publication © 1999
Second Edition Revised - © 2012

## Novels

### The Man in My Heart (A Mini-Novel)
The Sneed-Carter Christian Publication © 2009

# Table of Contents

## Thoughts of the Day

~

# Wisdom Moments

~

# Poems & Writings

~

# ~Preface~

Life is full of many challenges, trials, tribulations, and victories. There'll be times in our lives when we'll need encouragement and inspiration from, *"The Word of God"*, to help us make it from day to day on this Christian journey.

*Messages from Heaven* is an inspirational book full of rich wisdom nuggets: encouragement, challenges, and empowerment for the Body of Christ. I pray that this book is a blessing to all who read it! ~

*Anita R. Sneed- Carter*

*"It will be hard and rough, but keep making medicine for someone else. There are many in the faith who are weak and may stumble; even fall. But keep bearing one another's burden. Your strength in the Lord is medicine!"*

*-Anita R. Sneed-Carter*

# Thoughts

## of

## the Day

*"Let the word of Christ dwell in you richly, in all wisdom teaching and admonishing one another, in psalms and hymns and spiritual songs singing with grace in your hearts to the Lord."*

*Colossians 3:16*

# *P*urpose

*"In whom also we have obtained an inheritance, being predestinated according to the purpose of him who worketh all things after the counsel of his own will."*

*-Ephesians 1:11*

---

"Are you enjoying life and living purpose? God wants to work a mighty work in you and through you for his glory!"

"The next time you feel that your life has no worth remember this, *"God sees value in you"*!"

"You were not born by accident. Before you knew God, he knew you. You were created by design to fulfill God's purpose and plan."

"All were created to fit into God's plan. His plan and

purpose for your life is full of great challenges, and tremendous triumphs which will give him glory, and enrich your life."

"Do you trust God? Trust his *"Will"* in and for you. He does not make mistakes! He will not lead you in the wrong direction as you walk with him."

"As you come to know who you are in Christ Jesus, position yourself to know all he has for you through his *"Word"*, and become a great figure of action!"

# Thanksgiving

*"Let us come before his presence with thanksgiving, and make a joyful noise unto him with psalms."*

*-Psalms 95:2*

---

"Not one thing to complain about. In everything, we should always give thanks!"

"Will you give thanks unto the Lord? Giving thanks for all that the Lord has done releases a mighty praise!"

"When we learn to wait on the Lord for everything in our lives, we move to another level of thankfulness."

"Being in the presence of the Lord and worshipping him at his feet, ignites a flood of thankfulness and radical praise."

"Be careful not to take anything for granted. God does not have to bless us, but he does faithfully. Why? He loves us!"

"Continuing in thankfulness always, brings powerful humility."

*"Humble yourselves in the sight of the Lord, and he shall lift you up."*

*James 4:10*

# *P*raise

*"Because thy loving-kindness is better than life, my lips shall praise thee."*

$\qquad\qquad\qquad\qquad\qquad$ *-Psalms 63:3*

---

"Praise God no matter what type of day you may encounter. The praise will keep your spirit LIFTED!"

"When you begin to doubt, begin to praise. When you begin to praise God, reassurance makes itself right at home in your soul. Now send *"DOUBT"* packing!"

"Praise is the way to express your thankfulness to God."

"Have you had your praise break today? Be like David and dance a holy dance before the Lord. A praise break will send the devil on his way! There's a blessing in praising God!"

"For it is in the praise where you find your joy! It's a joy that's unspeakable in which the world did not, cannot give, nor able to take away."

"How strong is your praise? Let the strength of your praise come through the love of your heart and from the depths of your soul. Our God is worthy to be praised! Powerful praise produces a bountiful life!"

# *L*ife

*"But, as he who hath called you is holy, so be ye holy in all manner of life."*

*-I Peter 1:15*

---

"When faced with life's challenges remember to inhale the options set before you, and exhale the solutions from the Word of God into action."

"Live life and life will live in you, and through you!"

"What is your soul craving for the most? Is it right living? Or wrong living? Whatever you feed your soul the most, that's what you'll crave."

"Don't complain before you know. And when you know, don't complain!"

"Taking the time to smile at someone doesn't cost a thing. Share a smile today, and brighten the path of someone who needs a little sunshine."

"Finding a solution to a problem is not hard. It's just a simple challenge!"

"Making changes to one's life for the better is good. It will bring about present and future fulfillment. Staying stuck in a non-productive way can lead to a state of unrest!"

"We are not born with patience, but we are sure taught it!"

"Being kind doesn't cost a thing, but meanness does: the loss of a friend."

"Life is like candy and lemons. It can be sweet. Sometimes it can be sour. Issue out some sweet flavor for the world to savor daily, and good shall come unto you in return."

"Precious time spent well will make precious memories."

"It's another day that God has blessed you to be effective and productive. Will you be about the Father's business?"

"We are a precious and rare stone that has great worth, and powerful value. There's no price that can be put on us, because God encourages us to live our lives in such a way that our: husbands, wives, children, friends, and neighbors can see what holy jewels we are in Christ Jesus!"

"There will be disappointments in life, but disappointments should not stop growth. Let it make you more determined to succeed!"

"How much knowledge are you soaking up from studying the "*Word of God*"? Be like a sponge. Absorb all that you can, so that when you are squeezed, all that you have absorbed will flood out to others."

"What is passion? Passion is something that you desire the

most. Do you have a passion to serve the Lord?"

"Seeking God's wisdom during foggy days in your life will bring clear skies of knowledge, focus, and crystal clear understanding."

"A winner is a person of obedience and discipline!"

*"But grow in grace, and in the knowledge of our Lord and Savior, Jesus Christ. To him be glory both now and forever. Amen."*

*II Peter 3:18*

# Heart

*"Examine me, O Lord, and prove me; test my heart and my mind. For thy loving-kindness is before mine eyes; and I have walked in thy truth."*

*-Psalms 26:2-3*

---

"The heart is strong. Don't allow it to become weak. Give it exercise: FAITH!"

"Where is your heart today? Is it where it can be nurtured, or damaged? Watch out who you give your heart to."

"What's in your heart will come out of your mouth. Make sure what is in your heart is pure!"

"Want to know how strong your heart is? The more you

love the stronger your heart becomes. Exercise your heart with and in love daily!"

"It may be raining on the outside of your life, but the Son is shining on the inside of your heart. He's guiding you through those rainy days to dry land of victory!"

"It may be a cold morning, but ah! What a warm heart within! Can others feel the warmth coming from your heart?"

"Don't let any cold spirits chill your warm witness of the love of Jesus Christ. STAY FIRED UP!"

# *P*eace

*"And the fruit of righteousness is sown in peace by them that make peace."*

*-James 3:18*

---

"May God bless and keep you. May his arms of love wrap around you, and give you peace and fulfillment."

"Peace comes from the Lord. Have you tapped into the **Power of Peace**?"

"Having peace means having freedom!"

"Without peace in our lives, we cannot live a joyful life in Christ just as God planned it from the beginning of time."

"When you allow peace to move into your life the enemy Satan has to move out, because his thing is pure confusion."

"As long as your mind is stayed on Christ Jesus, you will be in perfect peace."

"Turn turmoil into peace. Speak it. It is done!"

*"For it is God who worketh in you both to will and to do of his good pleasure."*

*Philippians 2:13*

# God

*"Be still, and know that I am God; I will be exalted among the nations, I will be exalted in the earth."*

                                                        *-Psalms 46:10*

---

"Let God lead you into your path of "***purpose***", and you'll reach a dynamic place called, DESTINY!"


"You might not be able to see God, but you sure can feel him. He is ever present in our lives. This is truly good news!"


"God is serious about his love for you. Are you serious about your love for him?"


"God has time for you. Do you have time for God?"

"There is no one greater than the great *I Am*! Fear nothing. Don't fear anyone, because we serve an awesome and powerful God!"

"What seems impossible to us, God makes it possible!"

"Stop stressing! Remember to exhale. God has everything under control."

"There is no failure in God! Therefore, there is no failure in you. You are a child of the King, and that makes you a success story!"

"When you are honest with God, you then can be honest with yourself."

"If God does not change on what is right, neither should we."

"Giving God all of you means that you trust him with your life completely. Don't give him half. He wants you whole!

There's no one who can manage your life better than the Lord."

"Rest in knowing this, "God is the answer to and for everything"."

"Being in the presence of God is a humbling experience. Have you been in the presence of God this morning? It will start your day off right!"

# Encouragement

*"The Lord is my light and my salvation; whom shall I fear? The Lord is the strength of my life; of whom shall I be afraid?"*
*-Psalms 27:1*

---

"The more you grow spiritually, the more faithful to the Lord you become."

"Be encouraged. Stay in the race, because the *"Finish Line"*, is just ahead!"

"When facing a GIANT, don't back down. Stand tall on the *"Word of God"*, and the giant will be slain!"

"Satan will try to put the *"Plate of Disappointment"* on your table, but don't partake of it. Get up. Speak *"The Word"*, and the plate will disappear. There is power in the

*Word of God*!"

"Let nothing, or anyone hold you down where you can't fly freely in the joy realm."

"Smile no matter what, because it will uplift your soul, and to all who are around you."

"Encourage others through a word, or a deed, for it may be you who'll need encouragement tomorrow."

"Be warm, opened, and seasoned with and in humility. Many are watching you. Represent the kingdom in such a way, so that the world may see Christ Jesus in your Christian walk, and give God praise!"

"Stay in position where you can hear from God, and not Satan!"

"Whatever you do for the Lord do orderly, and with respect. Our God is Holy!"

"Regardless of how you feel at the moment, smile. A smile will take you a long way."

"Life may knock you down. Life may even leave you wounded severely. Pray to the Lord. He will pick you up, and heal all of your wounds. He will place you back on the track of life, and in the field to continue the race. You are a winner! Keep focused on the destination: HEAVEN!"

# *J*esus

*"Oh, taste and see that the Lord is good; blessed is the man who trusteth in him."*

*-Psalms 34:8*

---

"Need a new taste in your diet? Try Jesus!"

"The Lord is always patient with us without end. Can we be patient when waiting on him to answer, and move in our lives? Having patience is a sign that faith is present!"

"There is no one, or anything in this world that is better than Jesus. He is in a class all by himself!"

"Spend time with the Lord, and you will be blessed bountifully in spirit. Spending time with the Lord will be the best date that you'll ever have.   Let him be the lover of your life!"

"There is no love greater than the love of Jesus. With his love there is no doubt about, *"Will he ever stop loving me"*? His love is everlasting and unconditional. Who wouldn't want a love like that?"

"Let Jesus navigate your day today, for he is a great Captain!"

# Love

*"Beloved, if God so loved us, we ought also to love one another."*
*-I John 4:11*

---

"The love of God is like rain falling down on us; covering us with sweet flavor. Let his love season you!"

"Speak love, and not anger. Love produces action. Anger brings division and destruction. Therefore, speak love to one another. The Result: Love will come back to you!"

"To love God, is to know him. To know God, is to study his Word. To study his Word, is to grow your relationship. To grow your relationship with the Father, is telling the world how much he means to you. Question: How much are you in love with God?"

"Love is like pure gold. It never loses its value, or shine!"

"There is freedom in love, especially when it is unconditional."

"Searching for love should not exist, but letting love find you should."

"Walk in love today no matter where your feet may take you. You'll never know who will need it."

"If you give God all of you, every part of your life will be loved, nurtured and protected. That is his assurance!"

"Time is precious. It should not be wasted on things of no value. Make the most of your time. Love everyone that you meet with the love of Christ, and your time will be well spent!"

"We can't understand true love until we experience it!"

"Want to make God smile? Love one another!"

"True love is a richness that has no monetary value, but is a rich spiritual connection that is forever."

"Never turn away a helping hand of love. That helping hand just might be the very one in which God will use to rescue you in your time of need."

"The love of your life is the one who has your best interest at heart!"

# *Joy*

*"And my soul shall be joyful in the Lord; it shall rejoice in his salvation."*

*-Psalms 35:9*

---

"May this day be of great joy, and a bright spark for your soul. Enjoy this day and every day which the Lord gives."

"Face each day with humility, joy, and thanksgiving!"

"Happiness is temporary. Joy is ongoing! Which will you choose?"

# *L*ight

*"Let your light so shine before men, that they may see your good works, and glorify your Father, who is in heaven."*

*-Matthew 5:16*

---

"Don't let anyone try to dim your light. Keep it on HIGH BEAM!"

"The Lord's light never dims, nor can it be put out! It's so powerful it can brighten up the darkest places, and bring life to the deadest situations."

"Light will show up evil every time! Light is righteousness. Therefore, light and darkness cannot live together. Choose you this day whom you will serve!"

*"In the beginning was the Word, and the Word was with God, and the Word was God."*

*John 1:1*

# *F*orgiveness

*"And when you stand praying, forgive, if ye have anything against any, that your Father also, who is in heaven, may forgive you your trespasses."*

*–Mark 11:25*

---

"Forgiveness is simple, but is sometimes made to be difficult. It takes a strong individual to humble themselves, right or wrong to say, *"I'm sorry. Can we work it out? Yes! Let's work it out"*. Now that is maturity!"

"When you hold onto the past you short change your future. Let go of the things and persons who have wronged you. Forgive them. Release the past, and embrace your season of peace."

# *B*lessings

*"The blessing of the Lord, it maketh rich, and he addeth no sorrow with it."*

*-Proverbs 10:22*

---

"Reach up for your blessing. Reach out to be a blessing. The more that you give to others, the more the Lord will give to you. Keep the cycle going each day!"

"Have a blessed day! Make every moment count. And every second be of value. At the end of the day, count your blessings!"

"If you are always looking down you will always miss special things in life. There is a blessing in looking up!"

# *F*aith

*"Now faith is the substance of things hoped for, the evidence of things not seen."*

*–Hebrews 11:1*

---

"Walking by faith is a blessing, and helps you to grow. Be a *"faith walker"* every day. Your faith will get a real workout!"

"Keep the faith. Be obedient and a true rich blessing to one another. A faithful obedient giver is a picture of God."

"When faced with obstacles don't turn and walk away. Pray. Exhale. Have faith and jump over the hurdle. God is with you. Fear not! He will help you land on the other side of your "Red Sea", safe and sound."

"Having a tight relationship with God will give you tight faith! There will never be any room for doubt to creep in."

"Keep smiling and strength training in faith!"

*"It is not where you stand that makes an impression, but it is how you stand that makes a BIG statement; leaving a great impact. Continue to STAND firm for right. Leave wrong standing alone!"*

**-Anita R. Sneed-Carter**

# Wisdom Moments

*"Go ye, therefore, and teach all nations, baptizing them in the name of the Father, and of the Son, and of the Holy Spirit. Teaching them to observe all things whatsoever I have commanded you; and, lo, I am with you always, even unto the end of the age. Amen."*

*Matthew 28:19-20*

# Purpose

*"But seek ye first the kingdom of God, and his righteousness, and all these things shall be added unto you."*

*-Matthew 6:33*

---

If you are searching for a relationship with someone, try building one with Jesus Christ first. He will give you the tools you'll need to be all that you are purposed to be, do, and become. While you are loving Jesus, getting to know him, and letting him love on you, he is preparing your mate at the same time. Build a long relationship with Christ first, and the mate will be added. ~

# Thanksgiving

*"In everything give thanks."*

*-I Thessalonians 5:18a*

---

Arise each day with thanksgiving in your heart. Let praises flow like a river from your lips to God's ear with love. Let it come from deep within your soul; springing up with joy for all to partake. ~

# *P*raise

*"I will bless the Lord at all times; his praise shall continually be in my mouth."*

*-Psalms 34:1*

---

When Satan tries to get you off balance that only means that your blessing is right around the corner. Begin praising God! Satan doesn't like it when you praise God instead of stressing. ~

# *L*ife

*"Thou wilt show me the path of life."*

*-Psalms 16:11a*

---

Sometimes, it is hard to be faithful to all of your commitments. A Quick Revelation: "Don't commit to everything. Commit only to what you can do"! ~

Everyone has the right to be heard. But to be heard, one must speak in the right manner: with humility. ~

Turn away from anger, because it will only lead to destruction. Take time to reflect on why you are angry. When you have had time to think, you will perform the right action: a calm one! ~

Giving half of yourself to God says, *"I don't trust, or need you"*. When God gave his only begotten Son to die on the cross, he didn't give half of Christ. He gave all of him! If he would have given half of Christ, we would not be whole today.  Let God have your life. Trust him, for he knows what he is doing! ~

Every once in a while life will shake and rattle your foundation called, "***Stability***". It may leave a crack, but one thing it can't do, is break the spirit within you. Continue to stand firm on the "***Word of God***". Therefore, the next time your foundation has a light tremor, grab hold to the "***Author of Stability***", Jesus Christ! ~

Do you have your "***spiritual engine***" turned on? Are all cylinders running at full throttle? Be charged and ready for whatever comes your way this day. With joy and love inside of you, your full armor on, a smile on your face, the power of the Holy Spirit in and all over you, there is nothing that can't be won in Jesus name! ~

The formula to victorious living is simple: Obedience to God + Studying His Word + Faith = Victorious Living! ~

If you give your life to Christ, he'll give you life: eternal life! ~

Whatever and whomever is not giving you proper spiritual nourishment remove it and them from your life. You can't grow with unnecessary baggage weighing you down. ~

Every time you are kind to one another, you leave a spiritual legacy fruit behind for others to pattern after. ~

It's moving day! If you move yourself out of the way, God can then: work, strengthen, and bring great "*INCREASE*" into your life! ~

Why does God require things to be done decently and in order? He is for clarity, not confusion. Let's keep order in what we do for Christ in our: churches, jobs, homes, and wherever our steps are ordered by the Lord to go. The world is watching. ~

When one is puffed up with and in pride, they are in for a great fall. Pride destroys! ~

Don't let your sound judgment be turned into a weak moment. ~

Life is a map to different destinations. It can show us some pretty interesting places. Some are exciting, while others are frightening, and rather disturbing. There is one destination that is right on point with great beauty, peace, and fulfillment: HEAVEN! ~

A wilderness experience is only for a season. It's not a permanent destination. ~

Turning your life inside out is a really good thing, because you get a chance to see yourself, and not others. Realizing that change starts with you, helps one to bring forth true essence in this world that God has showered upon thee. Let the world see your inner essence: Jesus Christ! ~

When the Lord blesses you, sometimes, it is not to be told to others, because of their lack of being spiritually mature enough to handle it. Make sure that God says to share. If he doesn't want you to, then DON'T! ~

A friend is a true gift. When you find a real good friend, know that they are a precious gift from God. Cherish the friendship, because there are strong deep roots planted there! In other words, if God sent them to you, they aren't going anywhere! ~

Have you had your day of "*soul feeding*"? Feed your soul with the "*Word of God*" daily. It is the right food and nourishment for the soul; increasing spiritual growth, strength, and power from the Lord! ~

# $\mathcal{H}$eart

*"The Lord is my strength and my shield; my heart trusted in him, and I am helped. Therefore, my heart greatly rejoiceth, and with my song will I praise him."*

*-Psalms 28:7*

---

If your hand is closed shut, nothing can get in, or out. When your hand is open, you can give and receive. A Spiritual Look: If your heart is open to let love in, (Jesus), you will receive the greatest gift of all. If your heart is closed shut, you will miss the chance at "***Real Love***" and heaven. Give God your heart, and he will give you life! ~

With having a big heart, you will sometimes be hurt. Don't let that stop you from continuing to love people, because Jesus has a big heart full of love for us. When we're disobedient to his "***Word***", we hurt him, but he keeps right on loving us unconditionally. Love is a very powerful thing! ~

The heart is delicate, but is a very powerful instrument, and means a lot to God. Give your heart to him. Trust and believe that he will handle it with lots of care. It couldn't be in better hands! ~

May your heart be filled with love, passion, and the desire to do what is right towards others and yourself. ~

# _Peace_

_"Be perfect, be of good comfort, be of one mind, live in peace; and the God of love and peace shall be with you."_

_-II Corinthians 13:11b_

---

Live in peace and peace will live in you. Without it you cannot live, because peace is essential to success. God is peace. If you are without it, you can receive it. Just ask. ~

Don't let the storm in your life take control of you. You take control of it like Jesus did out on the stormy sea in the boat. He spoke peace to the storm. The storm stopped raging, and became calm. You have that same power within you: Jesus! Stop getting sea sick, and speak peace to your storm! ~

*"For nothing is secret, that shall not be made manifest; neither any thing hidden, that shall not be known and come to light."*

*Luke 8:17*

# *God*

*"We love him, because he first loved us."*

*-I John 4:19*

---

God's Word is powerful enough to change you quickly within. It is sustaining where others can see his power outwardly as a testimony of what he can do. ~

God will never give up on you, so don't ever give up on him! ~

Seek God's wisdom, for it is full of truth! ~

If you want to correct wrong, accept right. If what you do always seem to go wrong and never right, then try doing things God's way. ~

There aren't many assurances in life, but there's one thing for sure: God loves us! He shows us just how much everyday. God loves us in such a way in which no one, or anything can ever compare; UNLIMITED! He is in a class all by himself! Once you experience his unconditional love, you won't ever go back to LOVE LIMITED! ~

Giving God your time is a blessing. When you put him first, he will supply all that you need. ~

Keep reaching up and grabbing hold to all that God has for you this day, and everyday. What God has for you is good. It will be right on time. It's your season of bountiful blessings! ~

Putting everything in the Lord's hands says, *"I need you, and I believe you will fix everything"*. Trust God. He has you and your situation all in his hands! ~

# *E*ncouragement

*"Wait on the Lord; be of good courage, and he shall strengthen thine heart. Wait, I say, on the Lord."*

*-Psalms 27:14*

---

Go to church today, and have the *"Worship Experience"*. You may enter somewhat empty, but when you leave, you will be FULL! ~

Hold on just a little while longer. The risen Lord shall return soon! Truly, no one knows the day, nor the hour of his return in the clouds for the saints. We should be watchful, prayerful, and waiting.

While we wait, let us continue to share the gospel, and win many souls for Christ. Let's be about kingdom business. Soon you will hear God say, *"Well done thy good, and faithful servant"*! ~

Satan is on his job twenty-four seven. Why aren't we? He is trying to steal as many souls from God as he can. Let us put in some overtime, and reach as many souls for Christ as we can! ~

Have you ever had a sore that took a while to heal? As it began to heal, it began forming a scab; covering the past hurt. Then, as we sometimes do, for some reason, pick at it; keeping it from completely healing.

In life, whatever past wounds and hurts you may have, don't keep picking at them. Let full healing take place, so that you can enter into the future free, and with a fresh new start! ~

Be opened to new things, and your thinking will grow. ~

So many are hurting in many areas of their lives, but remember this, *"God is the best at bringing relief"*! Turn everything over to him. He can, will, and has worked it out! Be encouraged. Keep the faith! ~

Your circumstance is just that: a circumstance. It is not

your outcome! ~


Marriage is a sacred institution. It is work, but has great rewards! It has cycles: good and bad. Hang in there! Work it out together with guidance from God, through prayer, and the "*Word*". You will and can make it! ~


Keep pressing on toward the mark even when you don't feel like pressing your way through. Ask the Lord for strength to endure, and he will see you through all the way to the end. Don't give up!  Keep pressing your way, for your reward is in heaven. ~


When you exhibit patience, you're exhibiting GROWTH! ~

*"For we are laborers together with God; ye are God's cultivated field, ye are God's building."*

*I Corinthians 3:9*

# *J*esus

*"Therefore, if any man be in Christ, he is a new creation; old things are passed away; behold, all things are become new."*
*-II Corinthians 5:17*

---

When you come in contact with Jesus, you will not remain the same. There is a change on the inside that will be seen on the outside. You become a new creature, and old things are passed away. All things become new! If you are still feeling like the old you, it is time to talk to God. ~

When your car needs a tune-up, you take it to a mechanic. When we need a spiritual tune-up, we bring ourselves before the Lord, for only he can tighten up what is loose and rattling out of control. The next time that you are feeling like you are about to fall apart, take yourself to the *"Tune-Up Master"*: Jesus Christ! He'll fix you right up! ~

If you are running out of options, you have tried everything, and you are at the crossroads of "*Decision Avenue*" and "*Business As Usual Boulevard*", then try going straight ahead to "*Hope Street*". It will take you straight to Jesus Christ, "*The Hope, and Light of the World*"! ~

Turning from what is keeping you down and turning to who can: lift you up, dust you off, reshape, and mold you is a wise choice. Setting your feet on a path to "*purpose*" and a "*great plan*", is the GREATEST choice that you will ever make. Turn to Jesus! ~

# *L*ove

*"My little children, let us not love in word, neither in tongue, but in deed and in truth."*

*-I John 3:18*

---

Love is full of action. Not with a lot of talk. How much action are you sharing with the world where they can see love: Jesus Christ? ~

Taking the time to love others from the heart like Christ means that you are taking the time to give something that lasts. ~

Don't react to gossip, but rather let your silence be a witness to turn away wrong in love. When done this way, there will be a change, or cause wrong to find another portal for delivery. ~

Perfect love comes from perfection: Jesus Christ! You will never find a love better than, or that can compare to his love. ~

# *L*ight

*"Ye are the light of the world. A city that is set on a hill can not be hidden."*

*-Matthew 5:14*

---

Promises made are with a perfect glow that shines brightly. Are your promises glowing? Keep your promises, so that the glow continues to build TRUST! ~

Don't be shaken by what you hear and see on television about the economy, and the state of the world. God has everything under control! Things may seem dark, but remember, you have the light of Christ living inside of you! So, turn up your wattage, and help the world see *"HOPE"*: Jesus Christ, the Lamb of God! ~

# Forgiveness

*"If we confess our sins, he is faithful and just to forgive us our sins, and to cleanse us from all unrighteousness."*

*-I John 1:9*

---

No matter how far you have strayed away from God, you can always come home. There is nothing too bad that you've done in which he will not forgive you. God loves you! ~

While being crucified on the cross, Jesus asked his Father to, *"Forgive them, for they know not what they do"*. Being faced with great tribulation, Jesus was still teaching from the cross. He wasn't thinking about himself, nor his situation. He had the people and forgiveness on his mind, and in his heart. With that example from the "***Master Teacher***", the next time that you are done wrong: FORGIVE! ~

Forgiveness must be if you want peace. ~


Often times we hold ourselves hostage for the many mistakes that we have made in our past. Forgive yourself! Learn from your mistakes. Let it go, so you can grow and be free! ~

# *B*lessings

*"And let us not be weary in well doing; for in due season we shall reap, if we faint not."*

*-Galatians 6:9*

---

Be blessed. Not stressed. Whatever is not of God which tries to stress instead of bless, shake it off. Pack it under your feet, and walk in and with authority! ~

If you feel that you are about to give up at this very moment, here's a reminder, *"Hold on just a little while longer, because your breakthrough is on the way"*! ~

Let what we speak, speak life, and not destruction. Let what we speak be a blessing, and not a curse. The tongue is a powerful tool, and is sometimes unruly. Use with caution! Be encouraged to speak life to someone today, for it will enrich your life and theirs. ~


Obedience brings forth blessings! Disobedience to the ways of the Lord only delays your blessings. ~

# *F*aith

*"My brethren, count it all joy when ye fall into various trials, knowing this, that the testing of your faith worketh patience."*

*-James 1:2-3*

A promise is a covenant that is not to be broken. Once broken, it is hard to restore the relationship, and the faith. There is faith in a promise. Say what you mean. Mean what you say, my friend! God has never broken a promise, and neither should we. Before making that next promise, remember someone has faith in your words. ~

When trials and tribulations come into your life on this journey, "Will you run? Will you stand firm, and weather them"? Trials come to make us strong, and help us to increase our faith in God. Don't run. Don't give up. Stand!

God is testing and strengthening you. Be strong and stay encouraged, because you will make it through! ~

Give the Lord a praise offering, because you don't look like what you've been through! Your faith was truly tested, and you felt like giving up. But God! Your experience is a testimony that your circumstance is not your outcome! ~

*"Seek ye the Lord while he may be found, call ye upon him while he is near."*

*Isaiah 55:6*

# ℋeaven

*"For our citizenship is in heaven, from which also we look for the Savior, the Lord Jesus Christ, who shall change our lowly body, that it may be fashioned like his glorious body, according to the working by which he is able even to subdue all things unto himself."*

*-Philippians 3:20-21*

---

If you were planning a trip, you would make a list of things that you needed to do, or get. When tasks are done, you check them off of the list. The Spiritual Thought: Have you made plans for Heaven? Have you done what is required for Heaven? (Romans 10:9)? Is everything in order? Do you have your ticket stamped, "Salvation secured and Heaven bound; final destination"? There are no bags required. Flight for Heaven leaving soon! See you in the mid-air with Captain Jesus, for the *"**Rapture Flight**"*! ~

Spend time at the feet of Jesus in prayer and being taught.

When you get up, you can run this Christian race a little while longer, stronger, and wiser. You will grow spiritually. Your faith will increase. And with great zeal, win souls for the kingdom with the "*Finish Line*", (heaven), in view. This Christian race is not going to be easy, but it is worth it! ~

*"When the Lord disconnects you from your past, don't try to hook up with it again."*

*-Anita R. Sneed-Carter*

# Poems

# &

# Writings

*"For the Lord himself shall descend from heaven with a shout, with the voice of the archangel, and with the trump of God; and the dead in Christ shall rise first; Then we who are alive and remain shall be caught up together with them in the clouds, to meet the Lord in the air; and so shall we ever be with the Lord."*

*I Thessalonians 4:16-17*

# $\mathscr{P}$atience: From Stranger to Friend

*"And not only so, but we glory in tribulations also, knowing that tribulation worketh patience; and patience, experience; and experience, hope."*

*–Romans 5: 3-4*

---

Some days I feel like I know you.

Other days, you seem like a stranger to me, which makes it

hard for us to become acquaintances.

The question is, "Do I want to know you?"

You come with a headache, and sometimes anxiety.

Are you worth the wait, or bother?

Better yet! Are you worth the name that has been

bestowed upon you since the beginning of time?

On the other hand, Patience,

you can be a great friend who possess great

qualities, and benefits to, and for me.

You offer: maturity, experience, blessings, lessons learned,

strength, and endurance. I guess you have

grown on me. And just maybe, I do like you enough to

keep you around. I may even add you to my life's plan!

Therefore, stay! Hang around, and let's be real good

friends for a lifetime.

Let's make a go of it, shall we?

No longer a stranger, but a friend: Patience.


~

# *T*he Ants are Busy! Are you?

*"Go to the ant, thou sluggard; consider her ways, and be wise."*
                                                    *-Proverbs 6:6*

---

Have you ever sat down, and watched the steady

work ethic of the ant? No matter what obstacle get in their

way, they always seem to not let it hinder their work. Ants

will find another way around, or over the obstacle.

For sure, they work together tirelessly in harmony to

complete the task that the "*Queen Ant*" has assigned. Each

ant has a specific job. For example: Several may scout out a

location to build. Others work together to build the mound, while

others retrieve food. Several are assigned to defend the mound,

and so on, and so on.

Do you know what your assignment is in the

Body of Christ? Are you being slothful, and unconcerned

about finishing the assignment, or task that God has given

unto you to do? In Proverbs 6:6, it reads, "Go to the ant, O

sluggard, observe her ways and be wise." (NASB)

Why the ant?

Because they are a great example of how the Body

of Christ is to function in the church. Everyone in

the church has "*spiritual gifts*" that should be used to

help the church run smoothly. If someone is

slothful in their assignment, or even out of place doing someone

else's job, it will cause the body

not to function properly. The reference to a "**sluggard**"

means: a person who is lazy, or idle. You can't build up the

kingdom, and winning souls for Christ if you are idle!

Therefore, will you go to the ant,

and consider her ways, and be wise?

~

# $\mathscr{B}$EWARE!

*"Beloved, do not believe every spirit, but test the spirits, whether they are of God; because many false prophets have gone out into the world."*

*-I John 4:1*

---

In the last days, many will claim to know Jesus.

Say that they belong to him, and have been called by God

to preach the gospel. But beware!

How will you know if they are the real deal?

The Bible tells us how!

The Bible warns of this in Matthew 7:15-20,

"Beware of the false prophets who come to you in

sheep's clothing, but inwardly are ravenous wolves.

You will know them by their fruits. Grapes are not gathered

from thorn bushes, nor figs from thistles, are they? Even so,

every good tree bears good fruit; but the rotten tree bears

bad fruit. A good tree can not produce bad fruit, nor can a rotten tree produce good fruit. Every tree that does not bear good fruit is cut down, and thrown into the fire."

So then, listen to the message that they deliver. Observe the way that they live, and carry themselves publicly, and privately. What is in them will come out! If their fruit is rotten fruit, God will reveal it, and it will be shown to the world. With the light shining on them, it will either draw them to stop playing with God, and get real with him. Or it will send them away into seclusion where they can't hurt anyone again. If he chooses, God can and will simply remove them from existence through death.

Those who are truly called by the Lord to deliver "*His Word*", will produce good fruit! Jesus is shining so brightly in them that many will come to repentance after hearing the "*Good News*": The Death, Burial and Resurrection of our Lord and Savior Jesus Christ, and his return in the mid-air for the church soon one day! The Good fruit of the chosen and

called will promote Jesus, and not themselves!

Therefore, study the Word, be watchful, and pray that all

will come to know the truth.

BEWARE!

~

# $\mathcal{H}$ope

---

Hope is living.

Without hope, one would shrivel up, and waste away.

But living in hope, one will prosper in the richness of:

joy, love, peace, forgiveness, patience,

kindness, and understanding.

And what a rich intake that is!

So, live in hope. And let hope live in you

for the richness that it offers to all.

You will never be poor again!

~

# Why am I here, anyway?

It's another sunrise,

and I have a great view of all the things I'm to do.

But through the course of the day,

I somehow lose my way.

Then suddenly, finding myself about to say,

"Why am I here, anyway?"

I do understand, and know

we are all born with a purpose, for sure.

Some may be great, and some may be small,

but we are all called

to: praise, and worship God, love one another,

share the gospel, use our gifts and talents, be peace makers,

and help our neighbors here and abroad.

We will not leave this life until we've done all that God has

created and predestined us to do.

So, when you awake to another sunrise, and begin to say,

"Why am I here, anyway?"

Remember quickly, we are here on earth to do all things

God's way!


~

# $\mathcal{T}$he Smile of a Father

---

Remembering each day the smile of my father that told me
everything would be okay. When I looked upon his face I
saw the face of God, and God's amazing grace!


In heaven is where his soul now rests and resides
with that huge smile lighting up the sky. I will see him,
and that fatherly smile again one beautiful day,
in the sweet by and by!


~

# $\mathscr{A}$Tribute to Mother

*"Her children rise up, and call her blessed."*

*-Proverbs 31:28a*

---

Dear Mother,

Although you are no longer on this side of heaven, you are still in my heart. You left so much behind for us to treasure, that I really don't know where to start.

First, you gave me life, and nurtured me. Then, you taught, and lived before me how a: woman, wife, mother, and Christian ought to be. You showed me by example everyday how to: love, live, be free, and carry HOPE, (Jesus Christ, my Savior), in my heart truly indeed!

I will see you very soon in that beautiful place called, Heaven. It won't be very long! Until then, the memory vision of what a holy jewel you were is forever home in my heart. Your legacy truly has left a lasting sweet song! ~

# *K*indness

*"For with the same measure that ye measure it shall be measured to you again."*

*-Luke 6:38b*

---

Kindness is pure and clean.

O yes! On it, you can surely rest and lean.

Kindness doesn't know "***mean***", but

it knows all about the Jesus gene!

So, take a little time and live.

Kindness do show; the true gift give.

O what a thrill I know I feel,

sharing JESUS, the real deal!

~

# $\mathcal{T}$rifling Man, God is Watching You!

*"He that findeth a wife; findeth a good thing, and obtaineth favor from the Lord."*

*-Proverbs 18:22*

---

O trifling man with cut down character hands, you don't

have a clue of all the stupid stuff that you do.

God has given you a woman that completes, and

compliments you: outside and within! But the way

that you treat your gift is a total sin.

Wake up trifling man! You keep mistreating this ruby of

a jewel, she will be gone, and with another while your

passport to her heart won't be a renewal!

~

Anita R. Sneed-Carter

# ~About the Author~

---

American Christian Fiction, Inspirational, and Playwright, Author Anita R. Sneed-Carter, is a Texas native who has written several plays, and one Christian Fiction Urban Novel, *"The Man in My Heart" A Mini-Novel (2010)*, published by The Sneed-Carter Christian Publication. Her next novel, *"Diamond – Changed Forever" A Mini-Series*, will debut Spring 2013.

Mrs. Carter writes to encourage, inspire, and challenge one to live: **PURPOSE**, **POSSIBILITY**, and **CHANGE**! In each book, she births real believable characters with passion, riveting plots, and great storylines causing the reader to visualize living in the moments of each written word.

Anita lives with her family in the *"Lone Star State"* where she states, *"Life is simple, unique, and full of adventure"*!

~

*Jason Jefferson Falcone, a very vibrant, and colorful 16 year old orphan, is given a heavenly assignment which changes the hearts, minds, and spirits of the residents in the town of Diamond, Rhode Island. They are challenged to let go of color, race, and hate by now putting on the clothes of love, joy, and peace to experience God's grace and favor! This change brings about national attention, and touches the spirit of the President of the United States, Jimmy Gerald Scott Peterson, V. who is drawn to come, and be a witness to this awesome event.*

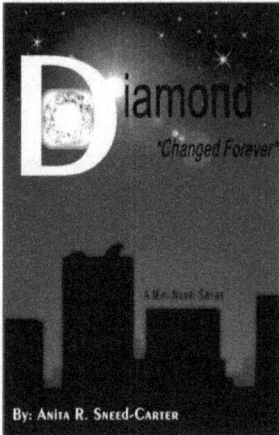

*Then suddenly, greater than the Diamond effect, the earth trembles, the sun brilliantly shines, and the clouds divide themselves! What will happen next?*

### COMING SPRING 2013!!!

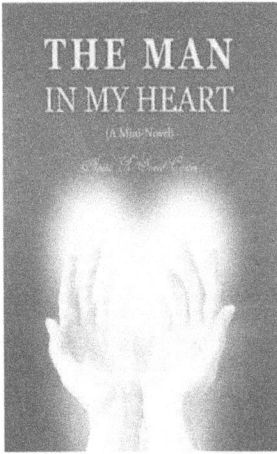

*American Christian Fiction, Inspirational, and Playwright, Author Anita R. Sneed-Carter, has done the unthinkable in the literary world by writing a novel with non-traditional editing on purpose, and publishing it to show the imperfections of an individual; "no one is perfect"! This method was chosen to aide in telling the story of her main character Valeesa Jackson-Prompay: a beautiful, successful broker located in Charlotte, North Carolina. Valeesa had it all, so she thought: money, power, prestige, a man, a mansion, cars, but later learned some valuable lessons from two con-artists that brought her to her wits end, and would cause her to run to her change.*

ISBN#-978-0-615-35088-2

Available wherever books are sold!

---

*"Wow! This book touched me in so many areas, and in a very profound way. It forced me, once again, to accept the fact that we humans are imperfect beings, and have no idea how to orchestrate our lives! I love the "out of the box" theme that you used as I have always been accused of being that way (smile). I too have made relationship choices based on what others perceived was best for me, and ended up hurt and wounded. This book reminds me of the importance of pursuing "God's plan" for my life instead of doing what is "expected" by others. Thank you for your realness and for not being afraid to address issues such as sexual relationships that the Church still doesn't feel comfortable addressing. I was so blessed and encouraged. I highly recommend this book to each of you. I heard God's voice from beginning to end. You must have this in your library!" ~ **Review by, Jamesina Greene the Author of, "Help, I Don't Like Myself!"***

*"Now unto him that is able to keep you from falling, and to present you faultless before the presence of his glory with exceeding joy,*

*To the only wise God, our Savior, be glory and majesty, dominion and power, both now and ever. Amen."*

*Jude v.24&25*